lillenas

PIANO
MODERATELY
ADVANCED

SUNDAY NIGHT Special

Gospel Favorites for Solo Piano

Lloyd Larson, Mary McDonald, Joel Raney, Jay Rouse, Heather Sorenson

Editor: Lloyd Larson
Music Engraving: MacMusic, Inc.
Cover Design: Ashley Donahue

ISBN: 978-0-7877-6010-6

PUBLISHING COMPANY

www.lorenz.com

Foreword

I was raised in a home and a tradition where Sunday night church was a part of weekly life....and that was a good thing! My parents would pack my four sisters and me into the car each week and off we'd go.

Sunday night church had a different "personality" than Sunday morning worship. The atmosphere was very distinctive. Everything was a little less formal (including the clothes I got to wear). There was more interaction between worshipers. The songs we sang were filled with joy; often more "testimonial" in nature as we sang about God's goodness and faithfulness. Sometimes our music minister would even allow us to request specific songs we wanted to sing in the service. As a child and teenager, I remember playing the piano and/or singing on numerous occasions. Several of my friends were invited to use their gifts as well in these services. Though this occasionally happened on Sunday morning, it was a fairly frequent occurrence on Sunday evening: *The Sunday Night Special.*

When we decided to proceed with this project to do a collection of some of these beloved gospel songs, I approached four of my friends – Heather, Mary, Jay, and Joel – who grew up in similar traditions to mine with Sunday night church experiences. They readily agreed to contribute. (The major challenge was narrowing this down to ten selections!) As you prepare and play these arrangements, you will quickly note that there is nothing here that dictates they be played on a Sunday night (or any other specific night, for that matter!). But I think you will quickly see why they got included in this collection.

These favorite gospel songs have survived the test of time. They continue to be meaningful and vital expressions of our faith. And I think you will enjoy the fresh settings each arranger has given to these piano solos. Our collective prayer is that you and those who hear you play these arrangements will find renewed inspiration in these enduring melodies of our faith.

—Lloyd Larson, Editor

Contents

About the Arrangers

Lloyd Larson is a freelance composer/arranger. His publications include over 1,500 choral octavos, Christmas and Easter cantatas, numerous keyboard collections, many vocal solo and duet collections, instrumental solo and ensemble publications, orchestrations, and handbell settings. He and his wife, Marci, live in the Minneapolis, Minnesota area. They have three grown children and four grandchildren.

Mary McDonald is a well-known composer of more than 800 choral anthems and many keyboard collections. She is published with every major publisher for church music and has had numerous top-selling anthems. Her unique blend of heart, hands, and humor, combined with a wide range of writing and performing styles has kept her in constant demand for nearly 30 years as a composer, keyboard artist, and as a choral clinician. A lifelong native of East Tennessee, she is married to Brian, and they have two married children and four grandchildren.

Joel Raney started playing piano sometime between learning to walk and learning to read. His broad musical interests have led to opportunities in many musical genres. As a composer and producer of commercial music, he has written soundtracks for more than 2000 television and radio commercials, plus numerous scores for short films. His sacred choral anthems, cantatas, handbell and piano arrangements, and instrumental works are consistent best-sellers. Joel and his wife, Susie, live in the greater Chicago, Illinois area with their three sons.

Jay Rouse's talents have taken him into countless venues, working with a wide range of artists. He has toured extensively in the USA and abroad with Sandi Patty as her Music Director and accompanist. Additionally, he has worked with Christian artists Bill and Gloria Gaither, the Gaither Vocal Band, Kathy Trocolli, Buddy Greene, and Veritas. He has created hundreds of choral octavos, numerous musicals and solo piano collections. He and his wife, Amy, live in Anderson, Indiana and are the parents of two children.

Heather Sorenson entered the church music industry a few years ago, and her name has quickly become recognized as a trusted and prominent contributor to church choirs and pianists across the country. She spends her time juggling a full writing load as well as traveling as a guest artist and lecturer. In her spare time, she loves catching up with friends over coffee, reading, and trying new-to-her restaurants. Heather makes her home in the Dallas, Texas area with her beloved (and very vocal) beagle, Lucy.

'Tis So Sweet to Trust in Jesus

with

I Surrender All

WILLIAM J. KIRKPATRICK
Arr. by Heather Sorenson

6

*"I Surrender All"

760106-6
*Music by WINFIELD S. WEEDEN

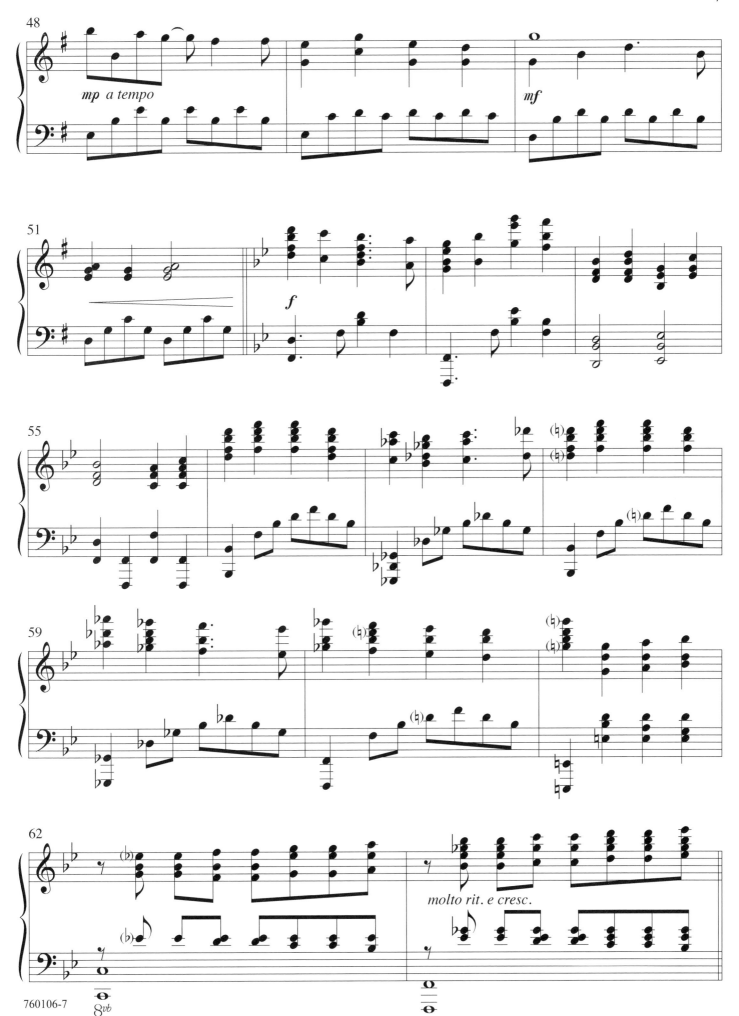

8

When We All Get to Heaven

EMILY D. WILSON
Arr. by Mary McDonald

PLEASE NOTE: Copying of this product is NOT covered by CCLI licenses. For CCLI information call 1-800-234-2446.

Love Lifted Me

HOWARD E. SMITH
Arr. by Joel Raney

Reflectively, freely ♩ = ca. 152 (straight 8ths)

What a Friend We Have in Jesus

CHARLES C. CONVERSE
Arr. by Jay Rouse

Warmly ♩ = ca. 120

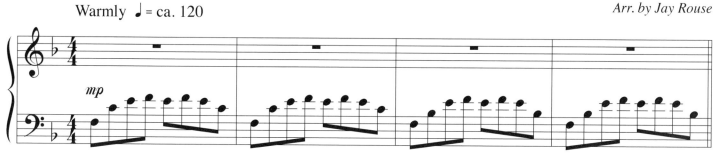

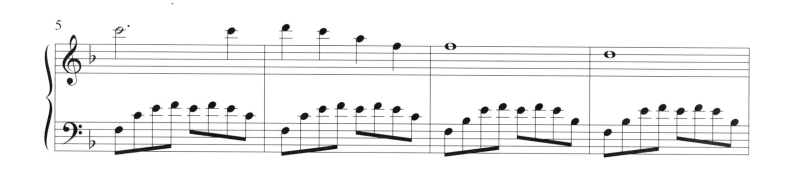

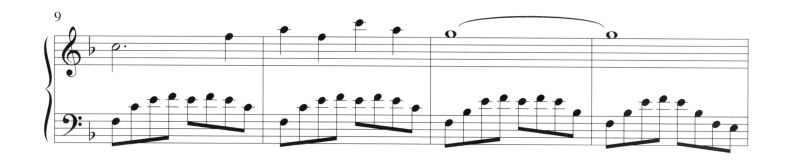

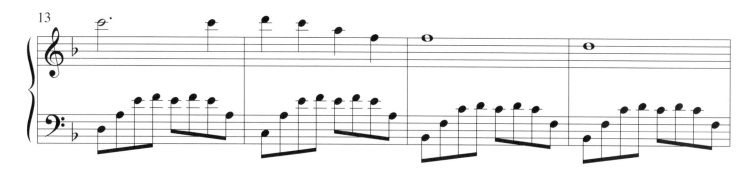

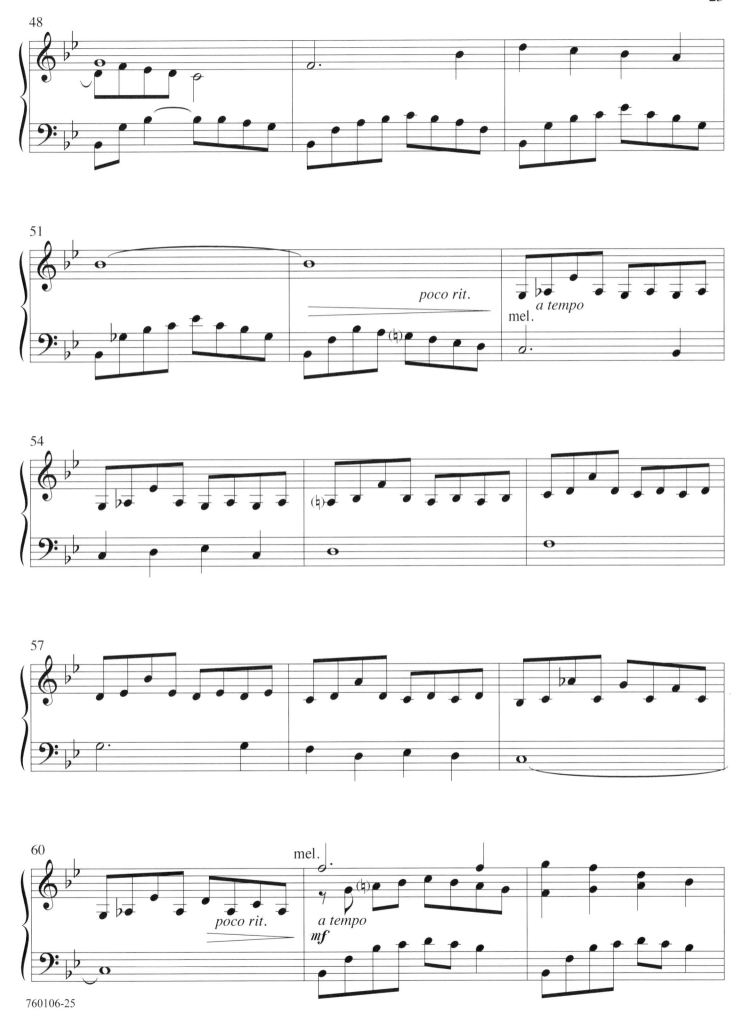

Satisfied

RALPH E. HUDSON
Arr. by Lloyd Larson

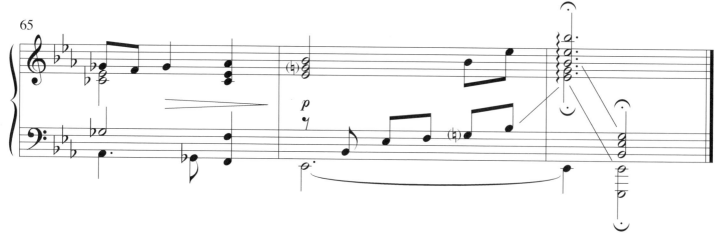

Sweet Hour of Prayer

WILLIAM B. BRADBURY
Arr. by Heather Sorenson

I Know Whom I Have Believed

JAMES McGRANAHAN
Arr. by Mary McDonald

Do Not Photocopy

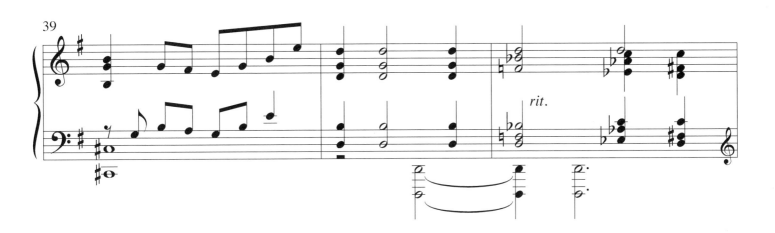

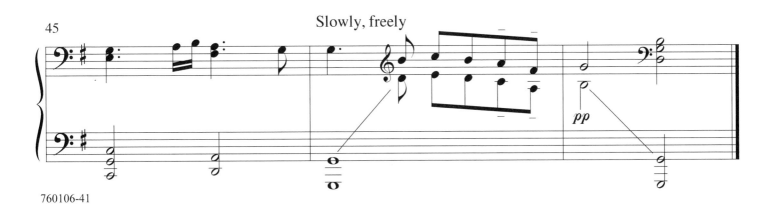

Sweet By-and-by

JOSEPH P. WEBSTER
Arr. by Joel Raney

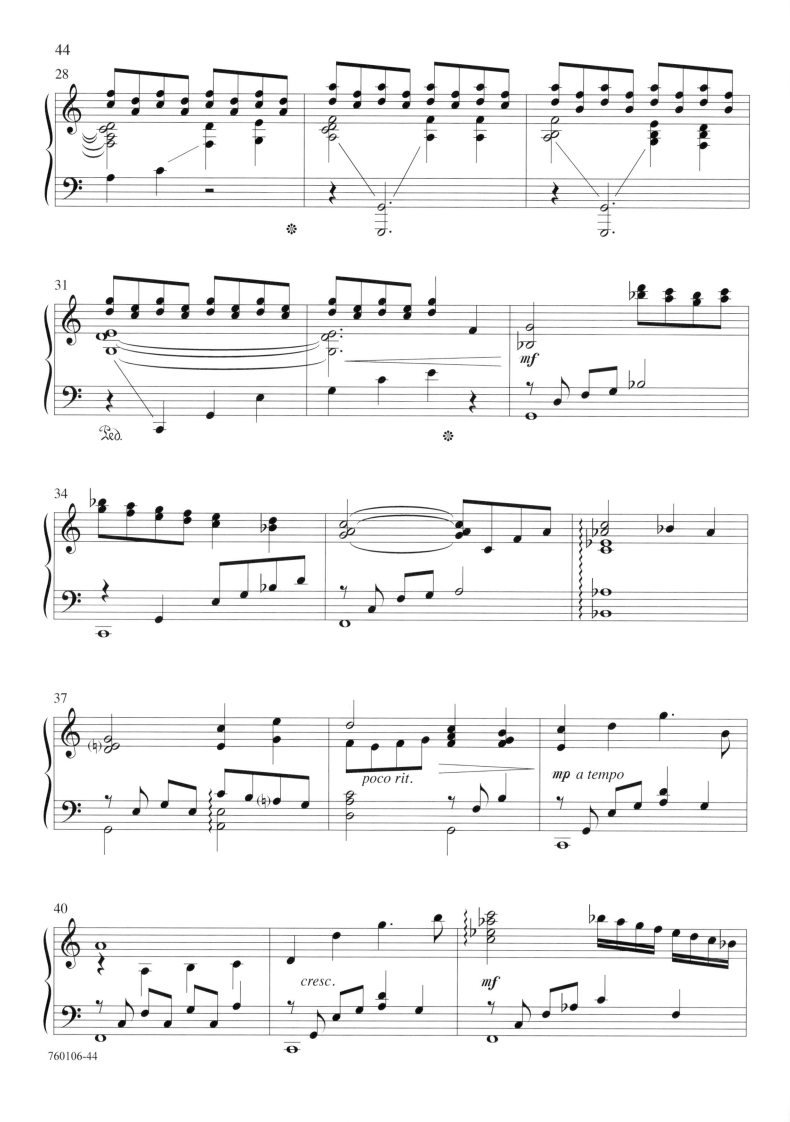

Playfully ♩ = ca. 108

He Hideth My Soul

WILLIAM J. KIRKPATRICK
Arr. by Jay Rouse

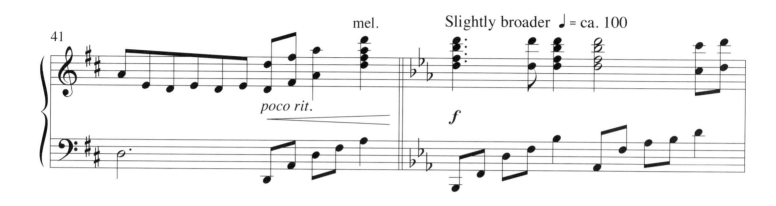

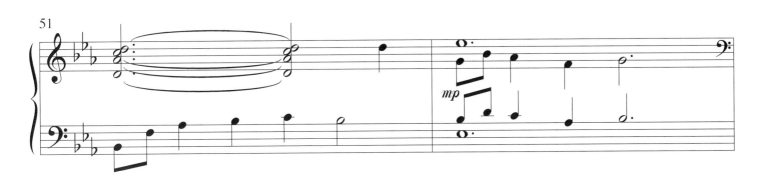

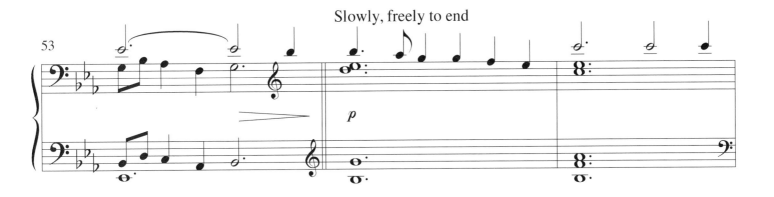

Slowly, freely to end

Trust and Obey

DANIEL B. TOWNER
Arr. by Lloyd Larson

Gently, steadily ♩ = ca. 116

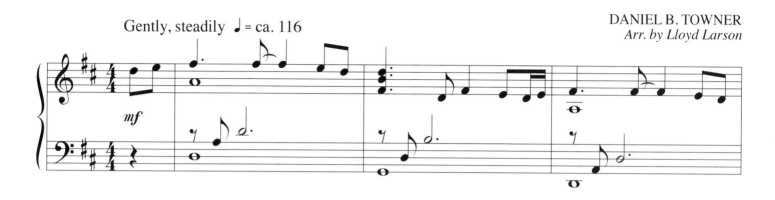

PLEASE NOTE: Copying of this product is NOT covered by CCLI licenses. For CCLI information call 1-800-234-2446.

56

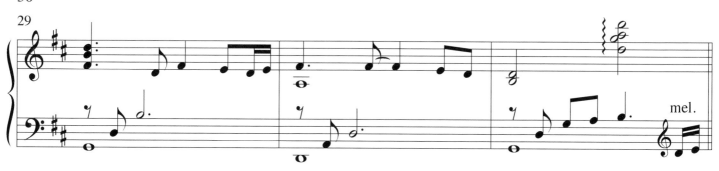

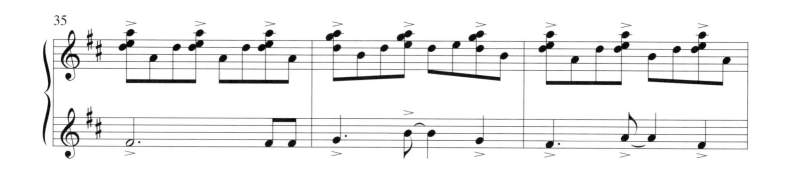